CONSUMER HAPPINESS: THE GIVE & TAKE OF EMOTIONAL PRODUCTS

A CASE STUDY IN PHILANTHROPIC BRANDING

DOAN T. NGUYEN

ACKNOWLEDGEMENT

This research was supported by production houses (Passage Entertainment and Envisage Media), the artist communities in Queensland and New South Wales, the Schonell Theatre, and the artist and journalism communities in Vietnam. The research data analysis software and research assistance were funded by UQ Business School, The University of Queensland. The author deeply appreciates the artistic input from all cast and crew in the Home of Strangers (2009) production.

The author thanks valuable feedback from colleagues at the University of Queensland and the University of Melbourne as well as participants at exhibitions and presentations at the University of Queensland, the University of Melbourne,

UQ/Griffith joint research workshop at the Hyatt Sanctuary Cove, Gold Coast, Australia, The Writer Club in Ho Chi Minh city, Vietnam. The author gratefully appreciates the feedback from Professor Kay Lemon from Boston College, Dr Julien Cayla from University of New South Wales, and Dr Karen V. Fernandez from the University of Auckland, New Zealand.

CONTRIBUTION STATEMENTS

Although subjective well-being and happiness has often been mentioned in consumer research as the result of a giving activity, the philosophical meaning of "happiness" has not been sufficiently defined and well understood. This study uses Aristotle's Eudaimonian view and Waterman's (1993) psychological view to distinguish between hedonic happiness and *eudaimonic* happiness. Using the information from a professional cause-related feature film project, I propose the concept of an Epic Gift, a gift that requires several contributors to complete and is given to a group of people for momentous and philanthropic reasons. Because of its magnitude, the making and the consumption of an Epic Gift connects the commodity exchange, gift giving and sharing systems, and modify the boundaries between private self, professional self, and possession.

ABSTRACT

This study reports on a two-year ethnographic research project that focused on a cause-related professional feature film production in which the researcher participated as the film director. The feature film was made to support an orphanage and theatrically released in 2009. Findings from this research project build on and extend the gift giving literature. Specifically, this study proposes the *Epic Gift* system, connecting the commodity exchange, gift giving and sharing systems.

The Epic Gift requires multiple contributors to complete the gift for momentous reasons. The findings support the notion that each individual contributor conceives different meaning of the gift ranging from a materialistic gift to a *taonga* and, thus, plays both the giver and receiver roles. *Hau* and *gaunxi* largely govern the reciprocity in the Epic Gift system and, therefore, Epic Gift contributors might enjoy *eudaimonic* outcomes when they contribute, and suffer penalties when they escape the giving circle.

1

INTRODUCTION

*There was no red carpet at the film premiere. Instead, black and yellow is the theme of the launch as it appears in the poster and throughout the promotional campaign. There were hundreds of people whom I didn't know personally. An old man approached and said: "Thank you so much for making this film. It's a privilege to be at the premiere, being a part of the event"... I felt as if I would turn invisible if I could. At the conclusion of months of sweat and tears in the name of charity, I needed a moment of tranquility to savor an extraordinary feeling of being blessed. And thus, thank **you** for giving me a chance to give* (Director's interview – media release 2009).

If we could recall the last time we did something philanthropic, what would it feel like? Philanthropic giving or simply contributing to charity makes people feel good or even happy (Liu and Aaker 2008; Reed, Aquino, and Levy 2007). Would the happy feelings we experience from dropping change into a random donation box, or volunteering at a community fund raising event be different from those that we have from performing at a major philanthropic concert to raise funds supporting thousands of victims of a natural disaster? Waterman (1993) suggests that these happy feelings are different, and belong to a two different conceptions of happiness. The first conception is hedonic enjoyment and the second one is *eudaimonia* – both are positive subjective states that have important implications for the understanding of the consumer's activity choices (Ryan and Deci 2001; Waterman 1993). In brief, hedonic enjoyment refers to the positive affects that accompany getting or having the material objects and action opportunities an individual wishes to possess or experience (Kraut 1979). In contrast, *eudaimonia* is defined as the subjective experiences associated with doing what is worth doing and having what is worth having (Aristotle 1985; Kraut 2011, Waterman 1993, 2005). In other words, *eudaimonia* refers to the feelings present when an individual is moving toward self-realization in terms of developing his unique individual potentials and furthering his purposes in living (Waterman 1993, 2008). If we consider the philanthropic concert as a gift, the making of this gift engages a group of individuals who might choose to contribute to the gift for hedonically enjoyable experiences or to make a difference. Depending on the level of contribution and the expected return from the gift giving process, different individuals will experience different affective states ranging from negative emotions (Wooten 2009) to (hedonic) happiness (Liu and Aaker 2008) or *eudaimonia* (Waterman 1993).

This paper uses the context of a real-life professional feature film made to support a charitable cause. The project involved several professional artists; some performed for the experience, some performed for financial incentive and some committed heart and soul to the project without calculating any possible return. This paper contributes to gift giving literature (e.g. Belk and Coon 1993; Joy 2001; Sherry 1983; Giesler 2006) and sharing (Belk 2010), firstly by proposing the Epic Gift concept. Such a gift engages several individuals to assemble different prototypes of a completed gift and reticulate it into the commodity exchange, gift giving and sharing systems. Secondly, this paper adopts the concept of *eudaimonia* (Aristotle 1985; Waterman 1993) into gift giving literature to understand the nuances in the emotional outcomes resulting from the involvement in the making of an Epic Gift. The emotional outcomes of such involvement could motivate the consumer to participate or escape the gift economy in the future (Marcoux 2006). Furthermore, understanding the Epic Gift system will have implications on consumer behavior research in self and possession (Belk 1988) and the negotiation between home (private) self and work (professional) self (Tian and Belk 2005).

CAUSE-RELATED ARTISTIC EVENT AS AN ETHNOGRAPHIC PHENOMENON

*C*ause-related artistic events (concerts, humanitarian films) typically feature popular performers working for little or no pay to contribute to an event as a gift to support a humanitarian, social or charitable cause. Recent large events related to important general causes were the Live 8 concerts organized by Bob Geldof and Bono and the Live Earth concerts organized by Al Gore and Kevin Wall on 07/07/07. There were similar events arranged following specific disastrous events such as the September 11, 2001 attacks on New York, the 2004 Indian Ocean earthquake, Hurricane Katrina in the US in 2005, and the earthquake in Qinghai Province, China in 2010.

Conventional models in the gift economy, however, are not sufficient to explain cause-related artistic events because these events are impactful, complicated and conducted on large scales. In addition, a network of passionate individuals is required in order to accomplish a sizable event. Because entertainment has the power to transcend social and cultural barriers and to move the world community to action, the integration of art, entertainment, charity and the people power behind each event converts the making of an Epic Gift into a consumption phenomenon (Live Earth 2011). For example, the concert led by the Hong Kong-born movie star Jackie Chan and performed by more than 100 Hong Kong and Chinese artists raised $4.8 million dollars to support victims of the 2010 Qinghai earthquake. The Live 8 concerts held in 8 cities around the world. These concerts were part of a campaign to persuade G8 member governments to increase their fight to eradicate poverty in third-world countries. Hosted on seven continents and broadcast in 132 countries, these concerts inspired 2 billion people worldwide to engage with the issues and the solutions surrounding the global climate crisis (Live Earth 2011).

Before undertaking this current study, I obtained a qualification as a professional film writer and director at a respected film school in Australia. After graduating from the film school, I contacted a 300 children orphanage in Vietnam with a promise to help them raise awareness and support using a feature film. I promised the orphanage that I would make a professional fiction feature and promote the orphanage during the filmmaking process. In addition, I would donate box office revenues from charity screenings. While the film is not about the orphanage, I made a commitment that the plot would be scripted to align with the orphanages' image and value. With agreement from the orphanage's founder and support from professional filmmakers, family and friends, I made the film.

First, I wrote the original screenplay as a fictional drama, recruited a professional production cast and crew, and directed the film. I then contacted a group of journalists in Australia and Vietnam who later helped to promote the film and the orphanage. I completed the film and released it to cinema in 2009. The profile of the orphanage was consequently raised at both national and international level. I agreed for an independent writer to adapt the original screenplay into a novel to be published in Vietnam. This novel subsequently became a top ten best seller in that country in early 2010. I donated all proceeds from the novel to the orphanage in Vietnam.

During the process of making the film, I documented all field notes, captured behind-the scenes notes, interviews with cast and crew, press releases, and media interviews. Although this cause-related feature film clearly does not have the impact or magnitude of the Live 8 concerts, the experience of making this gift and working with a group of passionate professionals is an authentic attempt to understand gift giving, sharing, reciprocity, self and possession in a philanthropic context. Similar to the experience at *Burning Man* (Kozinets 2002) where individuals could temporarily escape the market economy, the filmmakers could temporarily live in the story world during the period of making the film and escape from the hard reality of a fame-driven entertainment industry. However, similar to the fandom associated with Star Trek (Kozinets 2001) this experience is a stigma for those individuals who contributed to the project and had reached *eudaimonia*. Unlike the experience at *Burning Man*, however, when one can leave the event behind, the experience of making this cause-related feature film will last for a lifetime.

3

THE EPIC GIFT SYSTEM WITHIN THE GIFT GIVING LITERATURE

*A*n Epic Gift is defined as a gift accomplished by several contributors who each contributes a unique part to the gift, and without which the gift is not completed. An Epic Gift is to be given to a group of people for momentous and charitable reasons, and the compulsive reciprocation is driven mainly by the *hau* – the spirit of the gift. The process of making, giving, receiving and reciprocating an Epic Gift constitutes a complicated Epic Gift giving network that connects the commodity exchange, gift giving and sharing systems. I will elaborate the Epic Gift system below.

Gift Giving and the Epic Gift System

To date, there are three major theoretical systems that explain consumer behavior in gift giving (Belk 2010). The first system is primarily economic and uses the utilitarian motives of equivalence and equality as the springboard for understanding giving behavior (Garner and Wagner 1991; Joy 2001; Sherry 1983). In a philanthropic context, this system explains common donation behavior where utilitarian material (money, volunteered time) flows from the givers to the receivers. In return, the givers will receive common gesture of appreciation and general good feelings (Liu and Aaker 2008, Strahilevitz and Myers 1998). The second system focuses on the symbolic value of the gift and on how giving strengthens and maintains relationships (Belk 1976, Belk and Coon 1993; Joy 2001; Otnes, Lowrey and Kim 1993; Marcoux 2009; Ruth, Otnes and Brunel 1999). The ultimate form of giving under this system is the perfect gift, a gift which the giver is motivated to give through personal sacrifice and a deep desire to please the receiver without an expected return (Belk and Coon 1993; Belk 1996, 2010; Carrier 1995; Derrida 1992; Malinowski 1978). The third system is sharing

(Belk 2010) in which the exchange process (give and take) does not conform to the conventional boundaries of gift giving. Sharing is a process of distributing what is ours to others for their use, and taking from others to use without required reciprocity and ownership transfer (Belk 2007). In addition to these three systems, in a different context, the consumer gift system explains consumer gift giving behavior as a sophisticated network that consists of three key elements, that is, social distinctions, norm of reciprocity, and rituals and symbolisms (Giesler 2006). The Epic Gift system intertwines into the commodity exchange, gift giving and sharing systems in three different modes (Table 1).

Table 1: The Epic Gift System

	Commodity Exchange	**Gift Giving**	**Sharing**
Prototype of The gift	Contribute to the gift for a fee or professional credential.	Contribute to the gift for a chance to make a difference.	Sharing resources to help complete the gift.
Roles	Gift contributor Opportunistic follower Gift beneficiary	Inspirational driver Gift contributor Gift beneficiary	Inspirational driver Gift contributor Gift beneficiary
Meaning	Materialistic gift	Materialistic gift Taonga	Materialistic gift Taonga
Reciprocity	Guanxi	Guanxi Hau	Guanxi Hau
Eudaimonic outcomes	Hedonic	Hedonic Eudaimonic	Hedonic Eudaimonic
Examples of typical production roles	Production assistants Director assistants Editors Camera crew	Executive producers Producers Directors Actors/performers	Executive producers Directors Key cast Key crew

FIRST, in a philanthropic artistic event, when artists charge fees for their contributions they operate under the commodity exchange system. There is no difference between performing at a philanthropic event and performing at a commercial event. Because their contributions comprise indispensable components of the gift without which the gift cannot be completed (e.g. lead singer, composer, lead actor, director, director of photography) they contribute to the Epic Gift giving system. Second, under the gift giving system, artists could perform on a pro bono basis. Pro bono service is a professional service performed free of charge or at a reduced rate to help others. In a philanthropic context, a pro bono service can be considered as a giving activity or a charitable donation (Arnold, Nguyen and Hartley 2011). Third, in artistic productions, it is common that people share resources. This sharing activity comprises various types of sharing ranging from familial style sharing (Belk 2007, 2010; Epp and Price 2008; Money 2007) to general sharing (Price 1975; Shalins 1972) and communal sharing (Belk, Groves and Østergaard 2000; Bodenhorn 2005).

For example, a production budget is a fixed and limited financial resource, which artists, production crew and everyone else share. Thus, an expansion in expenditures in the costume department might cause a contraction in the lighting department's or other departments' shares of the budget. Furthermore, people share physical space (e.g. stage, production set) for an extended period of time. The director is the 'parent' in the production family where everyone shares his time and skills. In a nutshell, during a production process, artists build a professional family; they work, eat and sleep together under the same roof. These activities constitute sharing (Belk 2010).

The Hau Driven Reciprocity

Mauss (1925) looks at the spiritual mechanism that obligates people to reciprocate in the gift exchange process. The term *hau* in the Maori culture means the spirit of things (e.g. a gift). The *hau* is not associated with a common materialistic gift. Instead, it attaches to a *taonga* – a treasured gift (Mauss 1925). Although reciprocity is the central concept in consumer gift giving literature (Belk 2010; Joy 2001; Marcoux 2009; Giesler 2006) this *hau* driven reciprocity is particularly important in the Epic Gift giving process. Thus, it is worthwhile elaborating further on the concept here.

Concisely, Mauss's (1925) interpretation of the *hau* driven reciprocity operates on an on-going cycle. Person 1 gives Person 2 a gift. Person 2 passes the gift to Person 3. Person 3 then reciprocates by giving the gift to Person 2. The spirit of the gift (*hau*) forces Person 2 to continue the reciprocation by giving the gift back to Person 1 because when Person 1 gives the gift, he has given a part of himself to Person 2. When Person 2 receives the gift, he receives part of Person 1's spiritual essence. The same applies to the reciprocal relationship between Person 2 and Person 3. Mauss believes that the spirit behind the gift obligates the exchange to continue, and that the cycle of obligation to give, receive and reciprocate might extend perpetually. In the Maori folk culture, failure to conform to the *hau* might result in illness or even death. In the modern giving context, however, the *hau* driven reciprocity has different implications.

An Epic Gift, although constituted by different components and made by many people, carries an overall holistic essence that motivates the existence of the gift. When consumers support a cause-related artistic event such as Live 8 concerts, they support the ideal of eliminating poverty in third world countries rather than donating money to a particular individual. This does not mean, however, that the Epic Gift system is impersonal and soulless. Rather, the system is a unifying form of different entities and beings that are fused together to justify the existence of a superior gift. In other words, the Epic Gift system is similar to the form of giving and reciprocity discussed in Atwood (2008), Bodenhorn (2005), and Godbout and Caillé (1998). Specifically, the *hau* driven reciprocity in the Epic Gift system reflects two distinctive characteristics of the Epic Gift: (1) the magnitude, and (2) the dual roles.

First, the Epic Gift requires many people to bring it to fruition. Once it is completed and given to a significant cause and to a group of more than one individual, the nobleness of the gift makes the individual self become relatively insignificant. For example, a famous producer in the music industry organizes a charitable concert performed by several famous singers to support victims of a tsunami that killed tens of thousands of people. The concert is an Epic Gift. The producer invites a famous singer to perform at the concert. If the singer accepts the invitation as an opportunity to work with this famous producer and expects a favor in return from the producer in the future, the singer's giving in this case is motivated by *guanxi* (Joy 2001). However, if the singer participates in the concert because of any of the following reasons, he is motivated by the *hau* of the concert: (1) the singer cannot individually create the concert with similar significant impact; (2) the singer's collaborative performance in this concert will have a larger phil-anthropic impact than his solo performances in other commercial concerts; and (3) compared to a financial donation, the singer's performance in this concert is more meaningful to him and to the receivers of the gift. In sum, it is the *hau* of the Epic Gift (the concert) that drives the giving process of this particular artist, and the magnitude of the event makes his individual performance become less significant to himself and to the receivers of the gift.

In addition, the magnitude of the disaster makes an individual's suffering become less signifi-cant (this varies depending on the individual). The support given to the tsunami victims from the public audience of a significant cultural event possesses a symbolic meaning that result in hope -

a broader, more impactful and more enduring feeling to the victims than a feeling of personal relief (Fredrickson et al. 2008; Snyder et al. 1991). Thus, in both scenarios of the givers and the receivers of the gift, the magnitude of the philanthropic cause mitigates the significance of an individual self, and magnifies the resulting emotional outcomes (Fredrickson et al. 2003).

Second, the dual role is distinctive to the Epic Gift. This is where the *hau* has the most influence. The singer mentioned above is invited to perform at this noble and famous concert because of his talent. Similar to the concept of an involuntary debt (Godbout and Caillé 1998), his talent is a 'gift' that he has received. It is a rare gift by which he has made his fame and fortune. Using his gift, he has taken the opportunity that otherwise could have belonged to someone else. To that extent, he is obliged to return the gift by the *hau*, and the charity concert is an opportunity for him to reciprocate. This is similar to the holistic view about the whaling captain discussed in Bodenhorn (2005). To be a whaling captain, one needs power, recognition, sizable hunting recourses and, of course, whales. A whaling captain then has to share the hunted whales with his hunting team and the community in the village although they do not participate in the hunting process. The whaling captain is responsible to repay the gift he is given by the whales. In other words, the whale has given itself as a gift to the community, and the hunting business is only a conduit to transfer the gift between different parties. The spirit of the whale forces the reciprocity in the whaling business. Although the whaling captain gives a proportion of his hunted meat to the community as a gift, he is the receiver of the gift himself (Belk 2010; Bodenhorn 2005).

At the other end of the spectrum, a high magnitude natural disaster typically claims numerous victims and creates large-scale destruction. Thus, receiving support will trigger a sense of obligation from individual victims to either pass on the gift to those who might need it more or become a giver later on. This process is the core of the compulsive reciprocity under the *hau's* influence. One has to give, has to return the favor, and has to pass the gift on. In sum, the *hau* driven reciprocity makes contributors of the Epic Gift play dual roles (both giver and receiver). Thus, from now on, I will use the term the contributor instead of the giver or the receiver when referring to the

Epic Gift system. Figure 1 depicts the mechanism of the Epic Gift system.

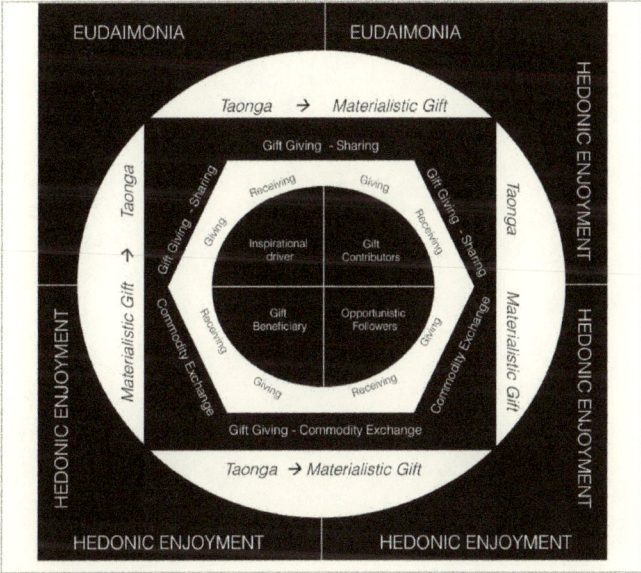

4

HAPPINESS AND EUDAIMONIA IN GIFT GIVING

*G*ift giving is a consumer culture theory that examines the formation and structuration of a moral economy – an economy where virtuous and moral behavior is rewarded (Arnould and Thompson 2005). Giving to charity is found to result in generally good feelings and happiness (Liu and Aaker 2008; Strahilevitz and Myers 1998). At a more symbolic level, giving a gift to a loved one would make an individual feel happy for the contentment of the recipient of the gift (Belk and Coon 1993; Belk 2010; Fischer and Arnold 1990; Joy 2001; Otnes, Lowrey, and Kim 1993; Ruth, Otnes and Brunel 1999). Research in social psychology suggests that giving and gratitude lead to happiness and well-being

(Emmons and McCullough 2003; McCullough, Emmons and Tsang 2002). In sum, giving is a virtuous activity to undertake and will result in wellness for the individuals via happiness and success (Lyubomirsky, King and Diener 2005). However, there is much more to happiness than that, as I will elaborate below.

Philosophical Views of Eudaimonia

Eudaimonism is an ancient Greek philosophy that postulates the principle of a human happy life as: "aretē" (virtue) constitutes *eudaimonia*". The term "eudaimon" is composed of two parts: "eu" means "well" and "daimon" means "divinity" or "guardian spirit". Therefore, to be eudaimon is to live well, protected and looked after by a benevolent spirit. However, despite this etymology, discussions of *eudaimonia* in ancient Greek ethics are often conducted independently of any supernatural significance (Kraut 2011). Instead, *eudaimonia* is a central concept in ancient ethical and political philosophy that implies a positive and divine state of being that man is able to strive toward and possibly reach (Aristotle 1985). The common English translation of *eudaimonia* is happiness, which does not capture the full meaning of the term. *Eudaimonia* is not simply a description of an individual's state of mind (Kraut 2011). In fact, Aristotle states that *eudaimonia* means *doing well* and *living well*, and it can only be achieved via the exercise toward aretē (virtue) and phronesis (moral wisdom) (Aristotle 1985).

This research adopts Aristotle's philosophical view based on three important reasons: (1) his account allows internal virtue (doing the right thing) to be accompanied by external goods such as money, career, power; (2) he suggests that hedonic contentment and virtues are necessary but not sufficient to attain *eudaimonia*; and (3) he states that to reach *eudaimonia* one should pursue a virtuous act only if it is worth doing and it flourishes one's excellence. Other influential philosophers' views on the same matter have been considered but not applied in this research (Pybus 1983). For example, Socrates considers that virtues (e.g. courage, compassion, justice) are both necessary and sufficient for *eudaimonia*. In other words, a person who shows compassion to others (e.g. donation to charity) cannot fail to be happy and a person who does not give to charity cannot be happy. For Socrates, a non-virtuous life is not worth living. Many other philosophers do not agree with this view (Parry 2009). From another standpoint, Plato suggests that if virtue goes against one's inner desire, pursuing this virtue will prevent the person from achieving *eudaimonia*. If a politician gives up an opportunity to win his election to champion a charity campaign that would improve the lives of many people, the success of the charity campaign might bring the politician good feelings. However, according to Plato, it robs him of a chance to attain *eudaimonia* (Parry 2009). This is similar to Aristotle's view on external goods. However, unlike Aristotle who accepts that without these external goods one cannot reach *eudaimonia*, Plato suggests that a virtuous person should not think about external goods at all. If career and power were not important to the politician, then losing his political campaign for the greater good would not prevent him from reaching *eudaimonia* (Kraut 1979, 1911). Clearly, this view might be adopted by some consumers who resist capitalism, but in this particular research context Platonism appears not to be applicable.

Psychological Views of Eudaimonia

Waterman (1993) is the first to apply the concept of *eudaimonia* to psychology and labels it personal expressiveness. Waterman (1993) states that while happiness is hedonically defined, the eudaimonic conception of well-being calls upon people to live in accordance with their daimon, or true self. *Eudaimonia* occurs when individual performs an activity which is most congruent with his deeply held values, and through the performance of this activity he feels intensely alive and authentic, existing as who he really is. Empirically, Waterman (1993) divides happiness into hedonic enjoyment and *eudaimonia*, where the former is necessary but not sufficient to achieve the latter.

Research in psychological well-being adopts a similar eudaimonic view describing well-being not simply as the attaining of pleasure, but as the striving for perfection that represents the realization of one's true potential (Ryff and Keyes 1995). If an artist is excellent at singing and singing is the activity he loves doing most in his life (his daimon), participating in a charitable concert (the Epic Gift) will give him an opportunity to help people in need (virtue) using his excellence (erete).

The magnitude of the concert, the recognition and the impact it has on people will give the artist a 'warm glow' feeling of being excellent (Waterman 2005; Csikszentmihalyi 1988; Csikszentmihalyi and LeFevre1989), being worthy (actualization) (Waterman 1993; Ryan and Deci 2000), being the best of himself, being who he really is, and at the same time being virtuous. That feeling is a description of *eudaimonic* feeling. The same artist could donate the money to a charity without performing. This donation would give him a feeling of hedonic enjoyment (Waterman 2005, 1993). Further, it could please him because he is fulfilling the six dimensions of human actualization (autonomy, personal growth, self-acceptance, life purpose, mastery, and positive relatedness) (Ryff and Keyes 1995). However, this contentment resulting from the donation is only a positive hedonic state of mind, not *eudaimonia,* because the artist is not acting in accordance with his daimon (Waterman 2005).

5

METHODOLOGY

he research presented here is from an ethnographic study that began in 2008. The study is in line with the process of making a feature film, including pre-production, production, and launch. The scripting and pre-production began in January 2008 when a full-length feature film script (120 pages) was developed. I worked with a professional editor for several weeks on the script. After 18 versions, the shooting script was ready for casting and production crew recruitment. I documented the recruitment of cast and crew in detail using videography and audio field notes. The formal auditions were videotaped by a crew. Other rehearsals and interviews on set were filmed on my personal camera.

During the actual filming process, there were two separate crews: the main professional camera crew and the behind-the-scene camera crew. The second crew documented all footage and audio material that I used for analysis in this study. The unprocessed footage of the behind-the-scenes runs for 70 hours and is stored in a 1TB external hard drive. Some edited behind-the-scenes were later printed in the film release DVD. Some practice footage was published on YouTube. There were eight photographers on the film set who took more than 500 photos, some of which were published on Facebook.

In addition to a 1 hour and 26 minute completed feature film, I kept all deleted scenes, behind-the-scenes, personal field notes, observation field notes, press interviews, media articles, email correspondence with cast, crew, comments and feedback from audience in email form, social media posts, hand written notes, mobile phone messages and a hard copy from the printed novel from Vietnam. The production consisted of 60 individuals cast and crew listed in the credits of the film. I did not use all of them as informants. I also interviewed family members and friends of the main cast and crew. I corresponded about the projects with key cast and crew for several months after the production was completed. Key informants are listed in Table 2.

Table 2: Profiles of Informants

Pseudonym	Age	Sex	Production role	Other occupation
Ann	55	Female	Ben's mother	Business owner
Ben	17	Male	Lead cast	Student
Chavonne	20	Female	Lead cast	Actress
Tom	42	Male	Props department	Business owner
Dean	20	Male	Supporting cast	Actor
Geoff	30	Male	Camera	Cinematographer
John	18	Male	Choreographer	Student
Leanne	20	Female	Lead cast	Dancer
Lee	51	Female	Catering	Business owner
Politian 1	42	Male	Endorser	Politian
Politian 2	30	Female	Endorser	Politian
Sean	56	Male	Producer	Business owner
Shera	65	Male	Script editor	Librarian
Soto	52	Male	Supporting cast	Spiritual practitioner
Stef	21	Female	Supporting cast	Actress/signer
Ted	27	Male	Music composer	Musician

THE DATA WERE ANALYZED FOLLOWING Thompson, Locander and Pollio's (1990) interpretive methodology. At the idiographic level, I attempted to gain some understanding about the meaning of participation in this cause-related feature film to these key contributors' lives. At a nomothetic level, I analyzed the material in great detail to find out whether or not similar patterns emerged for other participants. In this research setting, observation played a particularly important role. As the film director, I was the 'boss' of the production. People behaved differently when they were aware of my presence. However, as an artist on a film set, people came to me with their problems, issues, or concerns. When the filming was in progress, trust and bonding relationships between the actors and myself necessitated desirable results. This type of information was not revealed during an interview. Further, people did not purposely discuss their feelings or thoughts about the charity or the gift during the filming process. Thus, I relied on my observation and field notes to gain the information related to gift-giving behaviors that were not consciously or reflexively commented upon by informants themselves during the filming.

6

ETHNOGRAPHIC THEMES

The analysis results in three ethnographic themes in the Epic Gift system: (1) outcome driven roles; (2) shifting boundaries between self, possession and sharing; and (3) daimon and *eudaimonia*.

Outcome Driven Roles

Inspirational drivers. These contributors initiate, inspire and execute the Epic Gift project (e.g. producer, director, key performers). They are the most important contributors to the gift without whom the project would not occur or would not be completed. Inspirational drivers represent the Epic Gift in a public domain. The inspirational driver works at the level of the whole gift, whereas other contributors work at partial components of the gift. When the audience refers to the 'gift', they refer to the inspirational drivers.

"[Charity screening speech] This is not only a film, this is a vision of using an artistic product to convey a powerful humanistic message. This is not just an entertainment product; it is the work of courageous individuals ..." Politician 1

"[Personal commendation letter addressing the film director] It is fantastic to see individuals take action in response to injustice and further spread the word so more people can be inspired to help" Politician 2.

"[A letter from an audience member]... My mother and I had the opportunity to watch your film "XXX" at The Schonell Theatre today ...We would like to congratulate you and your team for your excellent creative effort in making this movie ... Your motivation for this movie for a humanitarian cause is highly commendable and we look forward to the release of the DVD of this movie...." Audience 1.

"[An email from an audience member] ... wow, I love the film, it was such a raw mix of love hate relationships. Congratulations for such a marvelous effort.

I am looking forward to the DVD release". Audience 2.

While Politician 1 addresses the filmmaking effort as a visionary philanthropic business, Politician 2 views it as a collective effort pulled together by the director. Audience 1 also sees the film as a collective effort of the team orchestrated by the director for a humanistic cause. In slightly different terms, Audience 2 sees more of the director's artistic attempts within the production than the cause-related nature of the film. Together, it is the film as a completed gift that the audience refers to via inspirational drivers.

Lastly, the inspirational drivers give reasons for the existence of an Epic Gift. As written by the orphanage's founder: *"There are many people who gave us the money. We are grateful of their generosity. But what you will do [making the film] gives us hope. The money might run out, but this hope will last us forever. I understand the risk of public objection. But in addition to the food that I feed my children every day, I have to give them hope as well. It's very important. So, please do make the film!"* That letter is the *taonga* to the producer and director of the film as it motivated and gave passage for the film's progress and for it to reach its destination. The permission from the orphanage was a gift, and it is the *hau* of the gift that carried the production through difficult times.

Gift Contributors. The majority of the people involved in making the Epic Gift were contributors. Contributors perceive their giving at different levels ranging from a materialistic gift to a *taonga*. Materialistic contribution is reflective of the conscious decision of their input and expected outcomes. For example: "*I couldn't believe I've gotten this far in the production business. I appreciate this opportunity so much. This is my first credit in a major role*" (Dean – supporting actor). "*Dean was so committed. He would get up every morning at 6am and yelled out his lines [the scripts] in the backyard. He wanted to make sure that he's ready for filming*" (John - choreographer). At the premiere, the only thing that mattered to Dean was that people would give him feedback for his acting. "*He doesn't even know that this film is made for charity, all he cares about is when it will become available and he wants to get a hand on the show reel*" (John). "*I can put this on the table and the agent can't say no to me. It's a feature film credit*" (Chavonne – lead actress). Unlike these contributors, Soto (supporting actor) took his contribution to a spiritual level. It was a *taonga* for him: *"I'm honored to be in this production. This is the first production I'm in since our move from the UK. And this is for a good cause. I'm so impressed with the whole thing. And all of that, it's got to result in good karma"*. The producer of the film commented at the media release: *"I did this project to support the young talent that I'm working with. It has been a journey on bumpy roads. I'm inspired by the commitment and dedication of the talent. It's all in the name of charity. But in the end, everyone benefits from it. Without the film, many of these young people will never had a chance to be in a proper production and will never had this kind of exposure"* (Sean - producer).

GIFT BENEFICIARY AND OPPORTUNISTIC FOLLOWERS. The orphanage is the obvious beneficiary of the gift. However, there are many other beneficiaries that are not so obvious. Contributors such as cast and crew who used the film for professional credentials benefitted considerably. In the entertainment industry, without experience (credits) cast and crew would have minimal opportunity to get paid work. Thus, early in their career, they accept free jobs to build their required professional credentials. To that extent, they are opportunistic followers and the beneficiary of the gift. For example: "*I don't want to sit on the wet grass. This is a $200 dress that I'm wearing. I don't want to ruin it. I'm not getting paid for this production, you know*" (Chavonne). This is a simple calculation. Sitting on wet grass, although it adds to the artistic aspect of the film, would not enhance her credit. She is an actress in a feature film irrespective of her sitting on the wet grass or not. Leanne lost her patience on set with multiple takes in a romantic scene: "*Come on, don't make any more mistakes, I have to wrap today, I have paid work to do!*" (Leanne). Similar to Chavonne, Leanne would compromise the production quality to rush to her next job. "*I need make up. I've never been in any production without wearing make-up. If this makes me look ugly then I can't use this for my show reel. So, what's the point of doing this film?*" (Dean). As mentioned above, Dean is a contributor who does not take into consideration the philanthropic aspect of the film. Unlike the two actresses, for Dean, the short-term payment is not even a concern. Dean would do whatever is best for his acting career and the feature film is a conduit for him to achieve his ambition.

SELF, Sharing and Possession within the Epic Gift System

NEGOTIATING PRIVATE-PROFESSIONAL SELF BOUNDARIES. Tian and Belk (2005) suggest the idea of negotiating for the boundaries between work self and home self in terms of possession that carries symbolic meaning of individuals' work attitudes and personal identities. The degree to which the extended self is revealed or concealed at work reflects a negotiation of the home-work boundary and our views of what aspects of our identity and lives belong to each domain. Analogously, filmmakers always negotiate the boundaries between private (home) self and professional (work) self. Professional identity is the work self which filmmakers use to psychologically register their contributions. During the process of making the film, individuals negotiate the boundaries between private self and professional self in accordance with their conception of the gift (e.g. a materialistic gift or a *taonga*)

One of the actresses wanted to separate her private possessions from items used in professional work: "*My boyfriend gave me these socks. I can't wear them in the film. I'm happy to wear anything else that you can find*" (Leanne - lead actress). On the contrary, another actress is happy to let go the boundaries. The voice of the mother via a lullaby sang by Stef was the key musical soul of the film. For the audience who understands Vietnamese, the lullaby performance was the tear drawing moment in the film. "*I left the vocal and pronunciation mistakes there on purpose. Zach's mother wasn't born in Vietnam, and didn't speak Vietnamese. To sing a lullaby like this, she's got to make mistake, you think?*" (Ted – composer). As the music composer of the film, Ted could improvise. However, although she does not speak Vietnamese, during the audition, Stef demonstrated that she is capable of singing the song in perfect Vietnamese. Stef agreed to portray the weak and soft voice of a mother singing a lullaby for her son in the film. To leave vocal mistakes in the production is a professional sacrifice for a singer/actor. However, that is a gift that she was willing to contribute to the production. At the same time, a famous musician requested that her name be taken off the production music credit, as her music was not used prominently in the film. She felt that the use of her music as a sub-sound track would influence her reputation negatively. While it appears that Stef was willing to contribute a *taonga* to the production, Leanne and the famous musician considered their contributions as materialistic gifts. Accordingly, while Stef voluntarily erased the boundaries between her private self and professional self, the latter artists preferred to reinforce the boundaries.

It was the second last shooting day when I received a call from Ben's mother that he was hospitalized and could not make the shoot. It delayed the production for two weeks. He could have taken longer, but Ben (lead actor) was determined to come back to the shoot as soon as he could. When he turned up at the shoot, he had lost significant weight when compared to his appearance in previous scenes. He was not fully recovered from his illness. Nobody on set noticed. As the director, I noticed the difference. I requested the choreographer to change the fight scene into a chase scene, where Ben only has to run around without fighting. "*I can't do that. I've spent weeks choreographing this. What make you think I can change it into a chase scene within half an hour?*" (John). "*We are losing the light if you don't hurry; the fight scene will be easier as we can do it indoors*" (Geoff

- cinematographer). The director has the final say. We had a chase scene, which resulted in one of the favorite shots in the film.

Behind-the-scene comments recorded by a second unit camera said: "*A couple of bruises and sweat, and so what? He's an actor; he should do whatever he is asked. My name goes with the choreography of the film*" (John). "*She cut all of my fight sequences out. I guess she's a director she can do whatever she wants, but this was supposed to be my scene, and now I traveled all the way for a two second scene presence!*" (Dean). At the film premiere, the script editor was not happy: "*You cut out a couple of my favorite lines and changed the characters around. There were several new scenes that I am not aware of. I didn't edit those scenes*" (Shera – script editor). In fact, there were more than a few new scenes, and the entire final sequence was changed.

Human being are primarily self-interested (Becker 2005; Malinowski 1922). Thus in professional filmmaking, contributors constantly negotiate for better shares within the gift. People such as Geoff, Shera, Dean and John care for the particular part that they are responsible for because it carries their professional identities. They possess these particular components of the gift. Thus, they are willing to contribute more to have a larger share in the production.

SHARING WITHIN THE EPIC GIFT. Sharing is a process of distributing what is ours to others for their use and taking from others to use (Belk 2007). Sharing does not require reciprocity and there is no owner-ship transfer (Belk 2010; Epp and Price 2008). Further, sharing goes hand in hand with trust and bonding between people (Belk 2010). Sharing out involves giving to others outside the boundaries separating self and other, and sharing in includes others within the aggregate extended self (Belk 1988, 2010).

During the film production, people share meals, accommodation, facility, equipment, and clothes (costume). Professionally, that sharing is necessary to complete the production and it can be considered as sharing out or professional sharing (Belk 2010). However, technically there is no social bond created by this type of sharing. After the production is completed, crew will typically go to other productions. Some will never work with each other again. However, there is evidence that sharing on a film set creates bonding relationship between individuals so that if they have an option to choose their future teammates, they will opt for a team with individuals with whom they have created bonding relationships before. *"I'd like to work with Dan [sound technician]; his equipment is very reliable and he has good ears"* (Geoff). As a cameraman, Geoff needed a sound technician to record sound professionally and separately from his camera. A sound operator such as Dan needs people like Geoff to provide quality images (pictures). Thus, Geoff and Dan shared out their equipment, sound and camera production teams, power source (electricity), radio equipment, monitors, and technical assistants. To accomplish this project, these teams needed harmonious sharing, not just ordinary collaborative teamwork. This sharing activity is similar to the communal sense of extended self in hunter-gatherer societies (Belk 2010; Woodburn 1998).

The film set is an extended professional family in which sharing is prominent. It is common to find dialogues discussing intimate matter about the character as if it happened in a real family. For example, *"[addressing the director] So, my wife and me wouldn't have had sex for a long time since our son died. Should I look at the chess set first then give her a kiss or do as the script says, kiss her and then play chess?*" (Soto). "*[addressing the director] I know the script says I push her down on the bed, but I think it feels better if she pushes me down*" (Ben). What Ben meant was the chemistry between the characters suggested that the female character would 'hit on him' rather than the other way around. Both Soto and Ben used their personal experiences (private self) to judge their on-screen relationships with their acting partners.

Conducting intimate scenes is one of the more difficult performances for actors, including experienced ones. It is when the boundaries between the private self the professional self (Belk 1988, 2010; Tian and Belk 2005) are ambiguous. While Ben had no issue sharing out with Chavonne by kissing her on set in an intimate scene, he has some concern with kissing Leanne on the cheek. "*[to Leanne] So, I'll just kiss you quickly on the cheek, then you go and wash your face ok?*" (Ben). "*You've got to do it right man, or we'll have to do it again!*" (Leanne). "*We just have to really kiss here. Just put the lips together but don't stick your tongue out*" (Ben). "*I can't kiss like that. Oh my boyfriend's going to see this!*" (Leanne). "*Yeah right, my girlfriend is going to see this too. But this is professional stuff, let's do it!*" (Ben).

[Recorded on production sound unit]. Chavonne is a professionally trained actress. For her, kissing is purely a professional performance. Ben and Leanne are not professional actors; thus, kissing for them feels as if they are sharing in with their intimate partners. Because sharing fluids dominant many prototypical sharing moments between sexual partners, and liquids nourish aggregate extended self when socializing (Belk 2010), both Ben and Leanne were concerned about how their actual intimate partners would receive the performances.

FILM AS POSSESSION. In addition to the fact that our possessions define and remind ourselves of who we are, (Belk 1988), the ambiguity of the boundaries between private and professional self (Tian and Belk 2005) in the filmmaking business inflates the social identity risks that artists could be exposed to. It is common in the industry that the actor's or director's name is associated with the production (e.g. Director X's film, or Actor Y's film). The artists' professional identities are associated with their professional credentials, and thus, reflect their social identities (Rydell, McConnell, and Beilock 2009) and create social stigma (Goffman 1963). Analogously, when a director or an actor makes a film, the work reflects his personal identity and social identity. If the film were considered as an Epic Gift, depending on how a contributor conceives the gift (e.g. a materialistic gift or a *taonga*) he would react differently to the reception of the gift. The more the individual's essence is invested in the gift, the larger the extended self (Belk 1988), and the more emotional (Fredrickson et al. 2008; Wooten 2009) the reaction will be.

We sent the completed version of the film to Sundance – a major film festival outlet for independent productions. It was a rush to make the 6pm postal deadline. The machine in the editing room had run non-stop for two days to print the film. It could not run any faster. We made it. After months of hard work, that was a major milestone. I came home with the disc and put it in my DVD player. Fifty-five minutes later, I sent the producer a mobile phone text message to let him know that in the major climax scene, the editing team inserted wrong footage from another film. That means when the film reached the climax scene, the viewers will see another film superimposed on top of this film. I refused to pick up my phone when it rang. Thus, I'd received five missed calls and a few voice messages: *"Come on, this is just a movie, nothing's personal, we'll fix it and send it else- where. I would come over and pick you up for a stiff drink, but I don't think you would even let me in the door. So. I'll see you tomorrow"* (Sean). *"It's O.K. I guess. We're not professional, and might never be in this production business. It's just a movie"* (Ben). I could hear a swallow of tear in Ben's message. This film was my first professional credential as a writer and director and Ben's as an actor. That submis- sion attached our first professional credentials to a broken film. While other actors did not react to the news, Ben's mother called the producer a few days later asking what happened that made Ben hide in his room for days. Ben's reaction to the news of the broken film suggests that the film is important to him and is a part of his extended self (Belk 1988). The broken film did not reflect his dedication to this gift. Presenting that broken film in public would feel as if his private self is distorted and negatively exposed to strangers.

Before the emotions from the technical hiccup subsided, the media hit. *[A local radio commentator] ... The movie is not as harmless as she [the director] claimed ... If she had a chance to make a movie, why didn't she make a movie about a hero? Instead, she made a movie about a gangster! She's got to be on to something [political agenda]! How could the community leader totally miss this action? We should organize a strike to prevent further screenings..."* And *"[Anonymous letter] ... these actors that you used are embarrassment on the street. They behaved like irresponsible and uncivilized teens. Why did you put them on the screen and put a price tag on them for charity? They're worth nothing. You either do charity or make a real film. Not both ..."* These comments completely erase the boundaries between private self and professional self of the filmmakers, treating the film and the filmmakers as one unifying self. Thus, in this case, the filmmakers were exposed to social identity risks (e.g. being labeled as 'philanthropic scam' or 'political opportunists'), and consequentially suffered from a high level of negative emotion.

DAIMON AND EUDAIMONIA

DAIMON. Everyone has a daimon within, regardless of whether he is aware of it or not (Aristotle 1985; Waterman 1993). Daimon is one's true self

(Waterman 1993) or one's excellence (Aristotle 1985). In a sense, it is one's talent – something a person is very good at doing, proud of doing, and loves doing. Some will be aware of his daimon and will live in accordance with it; some will never discover his daimon, or live in denial of his daimon. In either case, as agreed by all Eudaimonian philosophers, only when one can live in accordance with his daimon in a virtuous way, then one has an opportunity to experience *eudaimonia* (Aristotle 1985; Parry 2009).

Both Ben and Dean have talent or the daimon within them. In a film set, I as the director can ask actors to repeat a performance as many times as it is needed. I can ask for any kind of bodily and facial expression that I require to get the job done. However, ethically, I cannot demand the actor's emotional investment. As a 17 year old, socially popular, intellectually smart but lacking life experience, Ben turned up at the film set for one of the most dramatic scenes of the film – the gambling scene – apparently unprepared. I told Ben that the gambling scene was a "break it or make it scene" and that he did not look prepared. Ben naïvely responded: *"How could this one be that dramatic? It looks pretty easy. I only have to lose a poker game"*. I was disappointed with his interpretation of the scene. I asked Ben to go out for 10 minutes and re-think it. When he came back in, looking exactly the way he was before, I prepared myself for further disappointments. For the character in the film, that was the moment that he could be selling his soul to the devil. I said: "*action*".

"*The dealer flips the card. Ben looks at the last card, knowing that he has lost the game. He stares at the card for a few seconds when the camera moves from the right to the left. Strong spotlight from the ceiling pours down to the poker table and bounces back on the Ben's face. It was not a face of a 17 year old. It was a crumbled soul. There was no tear, no dialogue. It was just a few seconds of numbness*" (Director's note, the last shooting day, 2009).

I said "*cut*". The extra actor playing the dealer turned around and looked at me as if he was shocked with Ben's performance. Ben quietly sneaked off to a corner of the room. He faced the wall, but I could hear a very subtle sob, I knew there was a tear after I said "cut". What Ben gave me in that scene was not just a gift; it was a *taonga*, in which he invested his talent and a part of his soul to make it happen. He was not a trained actor; thus he would not know how to externalize a character. That means he has to invest his real emotions to produce the visible effect. I asked for the gift from Ben. I received it. Thus, for the *hau* of his *taonga*, I knew I owe him. A screen grab of the gambling scene is provided in Appendix 1.

Dean is a trained actor. In the final showdown scene on the film, Dean was required to perform a highly intense emotional act. Dean had been practicing the act for two months, and as the result, he did an excellent job. He could produce as many tears as I ask him to, and scream as many times as required. Irrespective of how emotional the scene was, after I said: "*cut*", he immediately returned to his normal self, laughing, joking and watching the replay of his footage.

On the contrary, Ben could never get back to his normal self immediately after an emotional scene and could not see himself in footage replay. I observed Ben several times during emotional scenes; by using his own emotions, he is vulnerable in front of his peers. In one of the emotional scenes, he asked me: "*Could I just have you and the crew in this scene?*" What he meant was he did not want to be observed by strangers if they were not absolutely necessary for the shoot. Ben did not need to rehearse, and in fact refused to rehearse emotional scenes. However, he performed excellently every time.

Both Ben and Dean were most happy when they were performing. I could see the pride in them after they pulled of a good scene. Performing is their talent and their daimon. Ben denies his talent and his daimon, but commits to pursuing a virtuous act. Dean lives in accordance with his daimon; however, it would not guide his action toward being virtuous. By contributing to an Epic Gift such as this cause-related film, Ben might be able to experience some form of *eudaimonia*, but Dean would only experience a high level of hedonic enjoyment.

EUDAIMONIA. Instead of the red carpet, black carpet and yellow balloons were used at the film premiere. Posters, picture, and press release articles covered the walls. There were many people. The ticket box was busy. There were many handshakes, praise, and laughter in the hallway at the premiere (Appendix 2). I was pulled between different groups of people for handshakes, conversations and autographs. Ben was nowhere to be found. The four hundred-seat theatre was filled with strangers. I was not sure what *eudaimonia* was at that stage, but I am sure I did not have it.

Dean walked around asking people for their thoughts about his performance. Chavonne was busy posing for photos. Ben reluctantly appeared at the end of the event because he suggested making a donation box to collect money for the orphanage. He gave some autographs, took some pictures and left quietly. There was not a dash of hedonic enjoyment on his face; there was certainly no *eudaimonia*. All I saw in Ben's face at the film premiere was anxiety. As Wooten (2009) points out, the anxiety of how a gift would be received could be so dominant that it would drive the giver out of the gift giving process (Marcoux 2009) and overshadow the positive emotions. For Dean and Chavonne, the contribution to the gift was materialistic. Compared to Ben, they contributed minimal emotional investment in this gift; thus they appeared to be oblivious of the charitable aspect of the film and how philanthropic communities might receive the gift.

At the third screening where Ben and I were invited to another city, Ben whispered during the screening: "*The last sequence was very well done*". After the first screening, the majority of the audi-

ence feedback and the reception of the philanthropic communities reassured us about the
film. *"Next time, if there is anything you need, just give
me a call. I'll call a gang for you within a day. What
you did is really important. Keep up with the good
work. Not many people have a chance to do this. You
did it. If you give this up, no one else in this community
will have a voice"* (Tom – art supplier). *"I don't care if
people like the movie or not. Look at all the hard work
that people put into it. No one deserves the right to say
anything nasty. If there was any humanity in people,
they wouldn't say anything nasty anyway. You have to
be proud of yourself"* (Lee – community supporter).
*"It was a well done film, characters were well defined.
But the most important thing about this production is
your courage in making it. Congratulations"* (Long –
film critic).

At the presentation after the screening, I finally
saw it in Ben: *eudaimonia*. He has gone past his
anxiety state, and could face his own images on
the screen. He was proud and happy. It took Ben
two years after his first encounter with the film to
accept the completion of the gift. I have never seen
him that happy, proud and full of confidence. At
that moment, I thought I have done the right thing
by getting him involved in the production – a once

in a lifetime experiences for him as he mentioned at the presentation.

Ben turned down an invitation to be in the second feature film. He was more aware of the philanthropic communities and his ethnic origin after making this film. He was more aware of his daimon and his excellence in art. He understood that denying his daimon by accepting an ordinary job would devastate him. However, to live in accordance with his daimon, he would have to commit to an acting career with no future in Australia. He accepted an ordinary life out of the limelight. He might have experienced *eudaimonia* during the production. To decide to give up his dream for a more practical life, he might never reach the state of *eudaimonia* again. If he had not been involved in the Epic Gift system, he would never have discovered his artistic daimon. Then he would not be penalized for not living in accordance with it. The *hau* of his gifted talent is penalizing him. When he turned down the invitation for the second feature film, Ben said: "*I would do more charity work to help people as long as it doesn't involve anything creative and emotional!*"

7

IMPLICATIONS AND FUTURE DIRECTIONS FOR CONSUMER RESEARCH

The Necessary Distance

THE EPIC GIFT consists of sizable artistic events that result in unique consumption experiences within the gift giving and receiving process. It allows consumer to give as little as a materialistic gift and receive hedonic enjoyment in return. It certainly accommodates significant contributions where individuals could subsequently experience *eudaimonia*. In other words, within the same completed gift, there is an allowance for various contributions and expected emotional outcomes. Research shows that the consumption context in charity could create reverse social effects due to social stigma and the social identity threats (e.g. supporting a charity reflects the social identity of the donors) (Argo and Main 2008; Berger and Heath 2008; Goffman 1963; Kozinets 2002; Small and Simonsohn 2008). Participating in an Epic Gift system gives consumer a necessary social distance because the magnitude of an Epic Gift mitigates the significance of individual self. Thus, individuals might be able to renegotiate the boundaries between professional self (Tian and Belk 2005) and private self (Belk 1988, 2010) to safely distance themselves from possible negative emotional outcomes.

The Making and the Consumption of Epic Gifts

THE EPIC GIFT system suggests that not all philanthropic activities are virtuous, and that not all virtuous acts lead to *eudaimonia*. Furthermore, attaining *eudaimonia* is not necessarily in the best interest of an individual if he cannot negotiate and balance the boundaries between private self and professional self. When individuals start negotiating and shifting boundaries between private self and professional self (Belk 1988; Tian and Belk 2005) to suit their best interest, the calculation will negate the nobleness of an Epic Gift (Belk 2010). However, without negotiating, key contributors of the Epic Gift system are vulnerable to negative emotional consequences (Wooten 2009) and could be forced out of the system (Marcoux 2009). To that extent, the system is not sustainable. Thus, it is important to understand whether negotiating boundaries between private self and professional self (Tian and Belk 2005) is the key activity for individuals to participate in a network of virtuous activities using their excellence and to enjoy an opportunity to experience *eudaimonia*.

Research on brand communities suggests that members of a brand community typically share a reverence for the brand, and thus are willing to share a branded joint possession to foster a communal sense of belonging (Muñiz and O'Guinn 2001) and solidarity (Giesler 2006). However, the majority of human beings are self-interested (Becker 2005; Malinowski 1922) including those who contribute to an Epic Gift. A number of informants in this current study appeared to be possessive of their contribution to the gift, and thus had a high level of emotional attachment to it. When individuals draw the lines between 'I', 'me', 'mine' and 'they', 'them', 'theirs' in the process of completing a major cultural product (e.g. a feature film, major musical event), is a collaborative ownership (Belk 2010) possible?

It is simple for consumers to purchase a product to support charity (e.g. stationery, household goods, raffle tickets) (Aaker and Akutsu 2009). It is also common for consumers to participate in fund raising events (e.g. sports, picnics, community activities) (Liu and Aaker 2008; Strahilevitz and Myers 1998). However, the consumption of a cultural product such as a film or a concert is not simple, especially when it carries the philanthropic aspect (Fisher, Vandenbosch and Antia 2008). Each individual artist possesses a unique set of personal and social identity (Denzin 2001; Heath, McCarthy and Mothersbaugh 1994, Holbrook and Grayson 1986). Consumers might share a reverence for the philanthropic project, but might not share a reverence for individual contributing artists. There are popular artists who are admired by an overwhelming number of fans (Argo, Zhu, and Dahl 2008). However, the artists' personal and social identities might not suit a philanthropic project (Forehand and Perkins 2005). Thus, it would be fruitful for consumer researchers to understand the extent to which consumer preference for individual artists affects their consumption decision of large-scale philanthropic cultural productions.

8

CONCLUSION

*A*n Epic Gift is a gift that possesses the following characteristics: (1) it consists of unique contributions from different individuals; (2) each contribution is associated with the contributor's personal and professional identities; (3) it exists for holistic and momentous reasons instead of individual dyadic relationships between givers and receivers; (4) it is governed by the *hau* driven reciprocity; and (5) it mitigates the sense of individual self and magnifies the emotional outcomes ranging from hedonic enjoyment to *eudaimonia.*

Everyone has a daimon within. The Epic Gift system allows individuals to contribute to virtuous activities to accentuate themselves and attain *eudaimonia*. However, without the balance between private self and professional self, the Epic Gift might have a reverse effect and *eudaimonia* might have a negative influence on an individual's psychological well-being. As pointed out by Bodenhorn (2005), having once been a whaling captain, it is not easy to return to a normal life as a businessman. Thus, while *eudaimonia* is the ultimate form of happiness that a human being could hope to achieve (Aristotle 1985) it does not come as a perfect gift, and should not be over-romanticized.

9

REFERENCES

*A*ll references used in this manuscript are listed below.

Aaker, Jennifer L. and Satoshi Akutsu (2009), "Why Do People Give? The Role of Identity in Giving," *Journal of Consumer Psychology*, 19 (June), 267-70.

Aristotle (1985), "Nicomachean Ethics" (T. Irwin, Trans.), Indianapolis, IN: Hackett.

Argo, Jennifer J. and Kelley J. Main. (2008), "Stigma by Association in Coupon Redemption: Looking Cheap Because of Others," *Journal of Consumer Research*, 35(December): 559-72.

Argo, Jennifer J., Rui (Juliet) Zhu, and Darren W. Dahl (2008), "Fact or Fiction: An Investigation of Empathy Differences in Response to Emotional

Melodramatic Entertainment," *Journal of Consumer Research*, 34 (February): 614-23.

Arnold, Stewart L., Doan T. Nguyen and Nicole Hartley (2011) "Pro Bono Service Sheds New Light into Commercial Friendship," *Journal of Strategic Marketing*, 19 (4), 381-94.

Arnould, Eric J. and Craig J. Thompson (2005), "Consumer Culture Theory (CCT): Twenty Years of Research," *Journal of Consumer Research*, 31 (March), 868-82.

Atwood, Margaret (2008), "*Payback: Debt and the Shadow Side of Wealth*," Toronto: House of Anansi Press.

Becker, Gary (2005), A Treatise on the Family, enlarged ed., Cambridge, MA: Harvard University Press.

Belk, Russell (1976), "It's the Thought That Counts: A Signed Digraph Analysis of Gift-Giving," *Journal of Consumer Research*, 3 (December), 155–62.

_____ (1988), "Possessions and the Extended Self," *Journal of Consumer Research*, 15 (September), 139-68.

_____ (1996), "*The Perfect Gift*," in Gift-Giving: A Research Anthology, ed. Cele Otnes and Richard

F. Beltramini, Bowling Green, OH: Bowling Green University Popular Press, 59–84.

_____ (2007), "Why Not Share Rather than Own?" *Annals of the American Academy of Political and Social Science*, 611 (May), 126–40.

_____ (2010) "Sharing", *Journal of Consumer Research*, 36 (February), 715-34.

Belk, Russell W. and Gregory S. Coon (1993), "Gift Giving as Agapic Love: An Alternative to the Exchange Paradigm Based on Dating Experiences," *Journal of Consumer Research*, 20 (September), 393–417.

Belk, Russell W., Ron Groves, and Per Østergaard (2000), "Aboriginal Consumer Culture," *Research in Consumer Behavior*, 9, 1–45.

Berger, Jonah and Chip Heath (2007),"Where Consumers Diverge from Others: Identity Signaling and Product Domains," *Journal of Consumer Research*, 34 (2): 121-134.

Bodenhorn, Barbara (2005), "Sharing Costs: An Exploration of Personal and Individual Property, Equalities and Differentiation," in *Property and Equality*, Vol. 1, Ritualisation, Sharing, Egalitarianism, ed. Thomas Widlock and Wolde Gossa Tadesse, New York: Berghahn, 77–104.

Carrier, James G. (1995), "*Gifts and Commodities:*

Exchange and Western Capitalism since 1700", London: Routledge.

Csikszentmihalyi, Mihaly (2000), "The Costs and Benefits of Consuming", Journal of Consumer Research, 27 (September), 267-72.

Csikszentmihalyi, Mihaly and Judith LeFevre (1989), "Optimal Experience in Work and Leisure," *Journal of Personality and Social Psychology*, 56 (5), 815–822.

Giesler, Markus (2006), "Consumer Gift System: Netnographic Insights from Napster," *Journal of Consumer Research*, 33 (September), 283–90.

Godbout, Jacques T. and Alain Caillé (1998), "*The World of the Gift*", trans. Donald Winkler, Montreal: McGill-Queen's University Press.

Denzin, Norman K (2001) "The Seventh Moment: Qualitative Inquiry and the Practices of a More Radical Consumer Research," *Journal of Consumer Research*, 28 (September), 324–30.

Derrida, Jacques (1992), "*Given Time: I, Counterfeit Money,*" trans. Peggy Kamuf, Chicago: University of Chicago Press.

Emmons, Robert A. and Michael E. McCullough: 2003, "Counting Blessings versus Burdens: An Experimental Investigation of Gratitude and

Subjective Well-being in Daily Life," *Journal of Personality and Social Psychology*, 84, 377–89.

Epp, Amber and Linda L. Price (2008), "Family Identity: A Frame- work of Identity Interplay in Consumption Practices," *Journal of Consumer Research*, 35 (June), 50–70.

Fischer, Eileen and Stephen J. Arnold (1990), "More than a Labor of Love: Gender Roles and Christmas Gift Shopping," *Journal of Consumer Research*, 17 (December), 333–45.

Fisher, Robert J., Mark Vandenbosch, Kersi D. Antia (2008) "An Empathy-Helping Perspective on Consumers' Responses to Fund-Raising Appeals," *Journal of Consumer Research*, 35 (October) 519-31.

Forehand, Mark R. and Andrew Perkins (2005), "Implicit Assimilation and Explicit Contrast: A Set/Reset Model of Response to Celebrity Voice-Overs," *Journal of Consumer Research*, 32 (December), 435-41.

Fredrickson, Barbara L., Michele M. Tugade, Christian E. Waugh, Gregory R. Larkin, (2003) "What good are positive emotions in crisis? A prospective study of resilience and emotions following the terrorist attacks on the United States on September 11th, 2001," *Journal of Personality and Social Psychology*, 84 (February), 365-76.

Fredrickson, Barbara L., Michael A. Cohn, Kimberly A. Coffey, Jolynn Pek, Sandra M. Finkel, (2008) "Open Hearts Build Lives: Positive Emotions, Induced Through Loving-Kindness Meditation, Build Consequential Personal Resources," *Journal of Personality and Social Psychology*, 95 (November), 1045-62.

Garner, Thesia and Janet Wagner (1991), "Economic Dimensions of Household Gift Giving," *Journal of Consumer Research*, 18 (December), 368-79.

Goffman, Erving. (1963), "*Stigma: Notes on the Management of Spoiled Identity*," New York: Prentice Hall.

Heath, Timothy B., Michael S. McCarthy and David L. Mothersbaugh (1994), "Spokesperson Fame and Vividness Effects in the Context of Issue-relevant Thinking: The Moderating Role of Competitive Setting," *Journal of Consumer Research*, 20 (March) 520-34.

Holbrook, Morris B. and Mark W. Grayson (1986), "The Semiology of Cinematic Consumption: Symbolic Consumer Behavior in Out of Africa," *Journal of Consumer Research*, 13 (December), 374-81.

Joy, Annamma (2001), "Gift Giving in Hong

Kong and the Continuum of Social Ties," *Journal of Consumer Research*, 28 (September), 239–56.

Kozinets, Robert V. (2001), "Utopian Enterprise: Articulating the Meanings of Star Trek's Culture of Consumption," *Journal of Consumer Research*, 28 (June), 67-88.

Kozinets, Robert V. (2002), "Can Consumers Escape the Market? Emancipatory Illuminations from Burning Man," *Journal of Consumer Research*, 29 (June), 20–38.

Kraut, Richard (1979), "Two Conceptions of Happiness," *Philosophical Review*, 87, 167-196.

Kraut, Richard, (2011) "*Aristotle's Ethics*", The Stanford Encyclopedia of Philosophy, Edward N. Zalta ed.

Liu, Wendy and Jennifer L. Aaker (2008) "The Happiness of Giving: The Time-Ask Effect," *Journal of Consumer Research*, 35 (October), 543-57.

Live Earth (2011) http://liveearth.org/en/liveearth, access Dec 2011.

Lyubomirsky, Sonja, Laura King, and Ed Diener (2005), "The Benefits of Frequent Positive Affect: Does Happiness Lead to Success?," *Psychological Bulletin*, 131(6): 803-55.

Otnes, Cele, Tina M. Lowrey, and Young Chan Kim (1993), "Gift Selection for Easy and Difficult

Recipients: A Social Roles Interpretation," *Journal of Consumer Research*, 20 (September), 229–44.

Parry, Richard (2009), "Ancient Ethical Theory", The Stanford Encyclopedia of Philosophy, Edward N. Zalta (ed.).

Price, John A. (1975), "Sharing: The Integration of Intimate Economics," Anthropologica, 17 (1), 3–27.

Pybus, Elizabeth M. (1983) "False Dichotomies: Right and Good," *Philosophy*, 58 (January) 19-27.

Malinowski, Bronislaw (1922), "*Argonauts of the Western Pacific*", London: Routledge & Kegan Paul.

Marcoux, Jean–Sébastien (2009), "Escaping the Gift Economy", *Journal of Consumer Research*, 36 (December), 671-85.

Mauss, Marcel (1925), "*The Gift: The Form and Reason for Exchange in Archaic Societies*," trans. W. D. Halls, New York: Norton.

McCullough, Michael E., Robert A. Emmons and Jo-Ann Tsang (2002), "The Grateful Disposition: a Conceptual and Empirical Topography" *Journal of Personality and Social Psychology*, 82, 112–27.

Money, Annemarie (2007), "Material Culture and the Living Room: The Appropriation and Use of Goods in Everyday Life," *Journal of Consumer Culture*, 7 (3), 355–77.

Muñiz, Albert M., Jr., and Thomas C. O'Guinn (2001), "Brand Community," *Journal of Consumer Research*, 27 (March), 412–32.

Reed, Americus, Karl Aquino, and Eric Levy (2007), "Moral Identity and Judgments of Charitable Behaviors," *Journal of Marketing*, 71(1): 178-93.

Ruth, Julie A., Cele C. Otnes, and Frederic F. Brunel (1999), "Gift Receipt and the Reformulation of Interpersonal Relationships," *Journal of Consumer Research*, 25 (March), 385–402.

Ryan, Richard M. and Edward L. Deci (2001), "On Happiness And Human Potentials: A Review of Research on Hedonic and Eudaimonic Well-Being," *Annual Review of Psychology*, 52, 144-66.

Rydell, Robert J., Allen R. McConnell, and Sian L. Beilock (2009), "Multiple Social Identities and Stereotype Threat: Imbalance, Accessibility, and Working Memory," *Journal of Personality and Social Psychology*, 96(5): 949-966.

Ryff, Carol D. and Corey Lee M. Keyes (1995) "The structure of psychological well-being revisited," *Journal of Personality and Social Psychology*, 69 (October), 719–27.

Sahlins, Marshall (1972), "*Stone Age Economics*," New York: Aldien de Gruyter.

Sherry, John F. (1983), "Gift Giving in Anthropological Perspective," *Journal of Consumer Research*, 10 (June), 157–68.

Small, Deborah A. and Uri Simonsohn (2008), "Friends of Victims: Personal Experience and Prosocial Behavior," *Journal of Consumer Research*, 35 (October), 532-42.

Snyder, C. R., Cheri Harris, John R. Anderson, Sharon A. Holleran, Lori M. Irving, Sandra T. Sigmon, Lauren Yoshinobu, June Gibb, Charyle Langelle, and Pat Harney (1991), "The Will and The Ways: Development and Validation of an Individual-Differences Measure of Hope," *Journal of Personality and Social Psychology*, 60 (April), 570-85.

Strahilevitz, Michael and John G. Myers (1998), "Donations to Charity as Purchase Incentives: How Well They Work May Depend on What You Are Trying to Sell" *Journal of Consumer Research*, 24 (March), 434-46.

Thompson, Craig J., William B. Locander, and Howard R. Pollio (1990), "The Lived Meaning of Free Choice: An Existential-Phenomenological Description of Everyday Consumer Experiences of

Contemporary Married Women," *Journal of Consumer Research*, 17 (December), 346–61.

Tian, Kelly and Russell Belk (2005), "Extended Self and Possessions in the Workplace," *Journal of Consumer Research*, 32 (September), 297-310.

Waterman, Alan S. (1993), "Two Conceptions of Happiness: Contrasts of Personal Expressiveness (Eudaimonia) and Hedonic Enjoyment," *Journal of Personality and Social Psychology*, 64 (4), 678-91.

Waterman, Alan S. (2005), "When Effort Is Enjoyed: Two Studies of Intrinsic Motivation for Personally Salient Activities," *Motivation and Emotion*, 29 (September), 165-88.

Woodburn, James (1998), *"Sharing Is Not a Form of Exchange': An Analysis of Property-Sharing in Immediate-Return Hunter-Gatherer Societies,"* in Property Relations: Renewing the Anthropological Tradition, ed. C. M. Hann, Cambridge: Cambridge University Press, 48–63.

Wooten, David B. (2009), "Qualitative Steps toward an Expanded Model of Anxiety in Gift-Giving," *Journal of Consumer Research*, 27 (June), 84–95.

ABOUT THE AUTHOR

Doan T. Nguyen is an academic at Swinburne Business School, Management and Marketing Department, Swinburne University.

This book is written as part of her on-going research projects on consumer social well-being, digital marketing for good, and the power of story-telling.

She can be contacted at doannguyen@swin.edu.au

www.ingramcontent.com/pod-product-compliance
Lightning Source LLC
Chambersburg PA
CBHW021155090426
42740CB00008B/1095